Quick&Easy

The
DOG, Owner's
Problem
Solver

Step-by-Step Techniques for Correcting Problem Behaviors

I0645754

tfh

Amy Fernandez

Quick & Easy®
The Dog Owner's Problem Solver

Amy Fernandez

**Quick & Easy® Perfect Puppy
Project Team**
Editors: Craig Sernotti/Mary E. Grangeia
Copy Editor: Stephanie Fornino
Indexer: Dianne L. Schneider
Cover/interior design: Stephanie Krautheim

T.F.H. Publications
President/CEO: Glen S. Axelrod
Executive Vice President: Mark E. Johnson
Publisher: Christopher T. Reggio
Production Manager: Kathy Bontz

T.F.H. Publications, Inc.
One TFH Plaza
Third and Union Avenues
Neptune City, NJ 07753

Printed and bound in China
09 10 11 12 13 1 3 5 7 9 8 6 4 2

Library of Congress Cataloging-in-Publication Data
Fernandez, Amy.
Quick & easy : the dog owner's problem solver : step-by-step techniques for correcting problem behaviors / Amy Fernandez.
        p. cm.
   Includes index.
   ISBN 978-0-7938-1011-6 (alk. paper)
   1. Dogs--Behavior. 2. Dogs--Training. I. Title. II. Title: Quick and easy.
   SF433.F38 2009
   636.7'0887--dc22
                                    2008053777

The Leader in Responsible Animal Care for Over 50 Years!®
www.tfh.com

Table of Contents

Chapter 1

Why Dogs Do What They Do

ontrary to what many people may think, dogs do not misbehave out of spite, they just do what's natural or what makes sense to them. In actuality, many of the things that we classify as problem behaviors are actually normal canine behaviors. But because dogs live in our world, we expect them to play by our rules. So for thousands of years they have modified their natural inclinations to chew, dig, and bark to coexist with us. However, this didn't happen without training—and their immense desire to please us.

NATURE VERSUS NURTURE

To change any problem behavior, we must first understand why dogs do what they do. Trainers and behaviorists speculate endlessly about canine motivations. Yet, despite these expert interpretations, it's impossible to read a dog's mind and truly know what he's thinking when he does things we find unpleasant or unacceptable. We can only make an educated guess regarding his motives based on the specific situation and his demeanor when he misbehaves. Once we can understand what a dog is trying to communicate, though, we can often redirect unwanted behavior toward acceptable positive behavior.

A DOG'S NATURAL INSTINCTS

Much dog behavior is directed by instinct. For instance, every dog circles around before curling up to lie down, whether he's on the living room sofa or a bed of pine needles. He also uses his nose to read details about the environment, whether he's at the vet's office or playing in the park. Every dog devotes a substantial amount of time to searching for food, too, whether he's well fed or starving.

Although these behaviors are inherent, unlike that of many animals, canine instinct is not rigidly programmed. Young or old, dogs constantly experiment, learn, and adapt to changing circumstances. This ability has been the key to their evolutionary success and the reason why humans have successfully trained dogs to accomplish so many amazing things for thousands of years.

Understanding your dog's natural instincts will help you train him effectively.

Understanding a Dog's Point of View

Because dogs are so intelligent, we've gotten into the habit of drawing conclusions about their behavior based on our own feelings. Dogs are clever, but they don't have the ability to plot, calculate, predict future events, or behave spitefully. It's human nature to interpret canine behavior from our point of view. It certainly complicates training when we ascribe human motivations to our dogs. On the other hand, this habit has led to an indelible bond between two completely different species.

Although you can't really know for sure what your dog is thinking, you can try to see things from his perspective. Dogs are very straightforward. In general, the most obvious explanation is probably the right one. If your dog nearly bowls over your grandmother when you walk through the front door with her, he's probably overwhelmed with happiness to see the two of you. To him, jumping up in greeting is the most appropriate way to say hello. He doesn't want to embarrass you or frighten Granny. You, on the other hand, might think that he's intentionally behaving inappropriately.

You may not appreciate this overly exuberant greeting, but you probably don't want your dog to leave the room and ignore you when you come home, either. To change his natural response, you must give him another alternative, along with the proper motivation to make that choice. This way he can decide to greet you in a calm, quiet manner whenever you bring your grandmother home for a visit.

Teaching Your Dog to Make Better Choices

Dogs constantly make decisions and modify their behavior based on changing circumstances. You can reinforce the behaviors you prefer through training. As a result, your dog will modify his natural behavior and make more acceptable choices. Humans have been molding the behavior of their canine companions for thousands of years, and there's no single method that works best. Every dog is different. Your training techniques should be tailored to your dog's personality, your personality, and your lifestyle. It's pointless to use a method that feels awkward to you or your dog, or one that requires far more time and expertise than you can muster.

QuickTip

Instead of scheduled practice sessions, incorporate training into your dog's regular routine. For example, ask him to sit when you prepare his food or watch television. Not only will this provide practice in a variety of situations, but these behavior choices will become a habit for him.

Basic Training Is Easier Than You Think

Many owners worry that training is extremely complicated and time consuming. In this book I will present a variety of simple techniques that can be easily utilized wherever and whenever they are needed. You will be surprised at what your dog can learn in five or ten minutes per day. It's quite possible that once you discover how easy and rewarding it is, you will be encouraged to try more complex training.

CORRECT COMMUNICATION

Successful training is founded on clear and consistent communication. Dogs are naturally responsive to humans thanks to thousands of years of genetic programming. But you must provide the right signals and motivations. Although you may not realize it, your dog learns from every interaction with you.

Paying Attention

The first step in training is to reliably teach your dog to pay attention. (See the "Pay Attention" sidebar on page 9.) After all, he can't learn if his eyes and attention are always wandering away from you.

Tone of Voice

Always use a consistent tone of voice when talking to your dog. Praise him in an upbeat tone. Correct him in

DidYouKnow?

Three weeks of daily practice will successfully modify most ingrained canine habits.

Most dogs are eager to learn, but it's up to you to help your canine companion learn the things that will enhance his life and enable him to live successfully with you.

a firm, low, quiet tone, and reinforce good behavior with a happy, encouraging tone.

Consistency of Commands and Body Language

Dogs can learn to understand many different words, but you must be clear and consistent when teaching them. Use a distinctly different word for every command so that your dog can easily differentiate them. Do not vary the phrasing—if you're teaching your dog to sit, stick with that term, and don't alternate it with "Sit down," "Sit stay," or "Sit good boy."

Consistency is equally important when communicating with hand signals, gestures, and facial expressions. Dogs are keenly aware of human body language, and they rely heavily on these clues when interpreting our training messages. Some trainers prefer using a clicker to reinforce training commands (see Chapter 2).

POSITIVE TRAINING FOR POSITIVE BEHAVIOR

Dogs constantly make decisions for clear-cut reasons. Many canine behaviors are instinctive or simply the result of long-standing habits. They are also motivated by the anticipation of a reward or the desire to avoid something unpleasant. For instance, every time you call your dog to come in the house, he must decide which available option is going to work out best for him. Maybe he should ignore you and lie in the sun or chase a squirrel in the backyard. On the other hand, if he comes in the house, maybe he will be rewarded with praise or a treat. However, the last time he came when called, he was scolded for coming too slowly and put in his crate. If you want your

Pay Attention

Begin teaching pay attention in a quiet environment with minimum distractions.

- Say your dog's name followed by a phrase such as "Look" or "Look at me."
- As soon as your dog makes eye contact with you, reinforce this with praise and a reward.
- Continue reinforcing the pay attention command long after he has learned it.

Dogs have excellent hearing, so if your dog isn't paying attention, you need to give him a reason to do this. Some dogs willingly work for praise and petting. For many others, you will need to use food as the primary reward.

Make Easy

dog to respond in the same way to a command, training has to be consistent and positive. Your dog should expect a positive response from you every time he performs reliably, in this case perhaps a word of praise or a pat on the head.

TAILORING TRAINING TO YOUR DOG

Knowing as much as you can about canine behavior and your dog's breed characteristics can be extremely beneficial during the training process because you can tailor your training accordingly. For instance, certain breeds, such as sighthounds, are more adept at reading visual cues. Others, like sporting breeds, respond more readily to praise as a primary reward. While being mindful of breed-specific personality traits that will influence your dog's response to training, pay attention to his own unique personality and style. Dogs require varying amounts of time and practice to learn specific concepts. Keep your expectations reasonable, especially if you're training a puppy. Many puppies look like adults at six months or a year of age, but mentally and emotionally they have a long way to go. Like children, they can be impulsive, energetic, and easily distracted.

Dog training includes its share of challenges, but these are far outweighed by the reward of mutual understanding and trust. Positive training methods also foster a much stronger bond between dog and trainer, and this is the basis for a lifetime of learning.

Chapter 2

Teaching Your Dog Good Manners

Dogs can learn unwanted habits very quickly, so it is important to remain aware of your canine companion's daily activities. Providing a structured schedule and consistent rules will offer him a solid foundation for basic good manners and may easily prevent most problem behaviors before they start.

PREVENTING UNWANTED BEHAVIORS

Your dog learns something from every interaction with you. He is learning when you feed him, brush him, and pet him. Even without formal training, he will learn to understand many words simply by watching and listening as you go about your daily routine. Because of this, training your dog can easily be incorporated into your everyday life. If you keep tabs on what your dog is doing, you can correct an unwanted behavior as soon as you notice it and show him what he should do instead. Likewise, you can consistently reward your dog for good behavior as soon as it happens. Proactive training prevents problems and revises unwanted behaviors before they become habits.

Your habits also play an important role in the training process. Not only must you keep tabs on your dog's behavior, but you must be aware of how your own behavior may affect your dog. You don't need to be directly involved in this. For instance, if your dog discovers a stray cookie when he jumps onto the kitchen table, he will probably continue doing this every chance he gets. To prevent habits like this, you must help him by not providing temptations. If unwanted behavior is not corrected or is inadvertently rewarded, in this case by constantly finding food on the table, your dog will probably repeat it again.

Experienced owners have a sixth sense about detecting and stopping misbehavior before their dog can follow through because almost every behavior is preceded by some clue about their intention. Interrupting your dog before he has a chance to misbehave will help him to understand your house rules, but you should also reinforce them by teaching him a few important lessons in good manners.

BASIC GOOD MANNERS

Every dog should understand basic commands like *come*, *sit*, *stay*, *down*, and *heel* (walking nicely on a leash). Familiarity with these concepts ensures

Providing a schedule and consistent rules will offer your dog a solid foundation for basic good manners and may prevent problem behaviors before they start.

that he will respond consistently and appropriately in a variety of situations.

A few minutes of practice every day will reinforce what your dog learns. Begin each lesson by getting his attention. This is an essential step in establishing and maintaining communication. Ask him to look at you, show him that you have treats, and make eye contact. This will ensure an effective training session.

SIT

With your dog on a leash, hold a treat near his nose and move it slowly over his head. Many dogs automatically sit as their head moves up and back to follow the treat. Even if that doesn't quite happen the first time, reward every response that is remotely correct. If your dog tries to grab the treat before he sits, tell him "No" and repeat the lesson.

If this doesn't work, kneel at his side, place your right hand against his chest, and slide your left hand from his shoulders to his rump to sort of gently tuck him into a sitting position while telling him "Sit." As soon as he starts to respond, reward him. Don't try to push him into a sitting position—most dogs instinctively push in the opposite direction. A clicker or hand gesture can also help reinforce the response. (See "Clicker Training" sidebar on p. 17.) Once your dog understands the *sit* command, say something like "Okay" to tell him when to get up.

QuickTip

> The process of introducing your dog to a consistent daily routine will familiarize him with important house rules.

STAY

Teaching the *stay* command is easy if your dog understands the *sit*. Attach his leash, use a treat to lure him to your side, and say "Sit." Instead of rewarding him immediately, wait three seconds before telling him it's okay to get up. Most dogs will automatically turn to face you before they stand up. This allows you to make eye contact to maintain his attention. If he starts to get up ahead of schedule, don't reward him. Either put him back into the *sit-stay* position or ignore him.

When your dog understands the idea of staying in place, gradually lengthen the time he remains in position and alternate long and short *sit-stay* lessons. You may need to up the ante on food rewards during this phase of training.

After your dog willingly sits for about 30 seconds, step back from him and see if he maintains the *stay*. Don't add this to the mix until he is reliable on the long *sit-stay.* Once he does this consistently, you can practice the lesson from varying distances.

For the stay, it's better to use a hand signal rather than a verbal command. Many dogs automatically get up when you say something or become confused if you add another word such as "come" as a release word from the *stay* command. *Come* is also a common command you'll use often. If your dog gets the idea that *come* and *stay* are interchangeable, you will have to start your training all over again.

DOWN

Many dogs are hesitant to lie down or stay down when excited or stressed, so make sure that your dog is relaxed when you start teaching this. Ask him to sit, hold a treat close to his nose, and slowly move it down toward his toes. His body will arch as he follows the treat, which should be in your hand and end up on the floor next to his paws. Some dogs lie down at this point and try to get the treat. If not,

Every dog should understand basic commands like *come, sit, stay, down,* and *heel.*

move your hand forward, just out of your dog's reach, and encourage him to stretch out. As soon as he is in a position approximating a *down*, praise and reward him.

Some dogs respond to hand gestures, like a downward sweeping motion, to reinforce the idea. A clicker can also help shape the response by instantly telling him that he's moving in the right direction, or you can click and reward the behavior every time you see him lie down on his own. Forcing a dog into a *down* position usually won't work and could be physically harmful. Most dogs reflexively push in the opposite direction and will stand up if you try to push them down.

COME

Your dog probably runs to you a million times a day when you call for him. Reinforce this behavior with praise or a clicker as soon as he starts heading in your direction. When he reaches you, immediately reward him with a treat.

Although your dog may come when called while indoors, keep him on a leash when first practicing this command outdoors—there are far more distractions and dangers. Practice, practice, practice in every sort of situation until you're 100 percent sure that he will never ignore you when you call him.

For more on teaching coming when called, see Chapter 10.

HEEL (LEASH TRAINING)

For leash training, use a light harness or collar that doesn't put pressure on your dog's neck. Use a special command ("Time to get dressed" or "Put on your collar"), and offer a treat whenever you put it on him. At first, leave it on for a couple of hours per day so that your dog becomes accustomed to it. After three days, attach the leash. Some dogs may struggle, sit, or lie down. Don't worry—this is normal.

Next, while your dog is on leash, encourage him to follow you with praise, treats, and squeaky toys. If he's having none of it, try again later. Give your dog time to get used to the idea of being on a leash and to learn that there's nothing to fear.

Leash training requires variable amounts of time and patience. Eventually, your dog will become bored and decide to walk with you. Trying to speed this up by pulling, jerking, or dragging him will only make him fear the leash and could harm his neck and throat. When he does start walking, encourage him with plenty of praise and treats.

Immediately start reinforcing the idea of walking at your pace on a loose lead rather than allowing him to pull or lag behind. Many owners wait until these bad habits are firmly established before trying to correct them, which is a mistake. When your dog strays, give the *heel* command, and show him that you have a treat waiting when he returns to your side. You can also stop moving entirely when your dog pulls. When he acts properly, start your walk again. He will eventually learn to associate walking nicely on leash with you continuing to move and pulling with you being completely still.

For more on leash training, see Chapter 8.

WAIT

Rather than responding to your dog's unruly demanding behavior, teach him he must behave properly before getting your attention by

Coming When Called

Although *come* is one of the easiest concepts to teach a dog, it's also one of the easiest to mess up. Here are some helpful tips:

- Never let your dog get into the habit of ignoring you when you call him.
- Never ask him to come if you're angry or planning something you know he dislikes, such as giving him a bath.
- Never forget to praise him as soon as he starts coming toward you, and reward him when he reaches you.

Make It Easy

DidYouKnow?

Puppies between the ages of 8 and 16 weeks are primed to learn vital social skills through positive contact with other pets and a wide variety of people. Regular interaction with unfamiliar people and places is important for your puppy's ongoing education and helps him to become a well-behaved member of his family and community. Taking him on daily walks, bringing him along on errands and visits with friends, or enrolling him in a doggy day care program are just a few ways to help him improve his social skills. Proper socialization isn't just for puppies, though. It should continue throughout your dog's life.

using the *wait* command. You can do this by asking him to wait and sit quietly before giving him his dinner, a favorite toy, your undivided attention, etc. Don't give in to barking or nudges. If you do, your dog will continue to use unwanted behavior whenever he wants something from you.

STAY BACK

Teaching your dog not to rush out of open doors can potentially save his life. To do this, put him on a short leash near a self-closing door such as a screen door. Open it part way and when he starts rushing out, tell him "Stay back" ("Wait" can be used here too) and let the door shut. Do this several times. When he hesitates and looks to you for permission before trying to barrel out the door, reward that response.

TAKE A NAP

Dogs instinctively retreat to a favorite spot to rest, and you can teach your dog to go there on command. Take him to his spot, use a phrase like "Take a nap," and give him a treat or a favorite chew toy. If he complains or gets up, tell him "No," put him back in his spot, and repeat the process until he makes the connection. Gradually increase the time that he's expected to stay there.

Clicker Training

Clicker training is an excellent method to incorporate into your training routine. It improves your timing when dispensing rewards and encourages your dog to form a positive association between a specific behavior and a reward. It also allows you to easily reward good behavior with precisely timed reinforcements. A click tells your dog when he has performed the correct behavior and that a reward is on the way.

This technique can be integrated into almost any kind of training, but it's especially effective for reinforcing straightforward commands like *sit* and *come*. Basically, all you have to do is:

- Click and immediately give a treat. Repeat this until your dog anticipates a treat every time he hears the click.
- Wait for your dog to perform the behavior you're trying to teach, such as sitting. Immediately click and reward him each time he performs correctly. Ignore incorrect responses.
- Repeat these steps until your dog makes the connection. This can take a variable amount of time. For some dogs, it helps to add a hand signal, like an upraised palm. But don't start combining clicker training with verbal commands until your dog performs the behavior automatically or in response to a hand signal first.

Make Easy

It's easier and faster to prevent bad habits and encourage good ones than to eliminate bad ones once they are established. So be careful to help your dog learn things that can enhance his life and enable him to live successfully with you. Think of dog training as a relationship rather than a chore to be tackled and finished. The process fosters understanding, communication, and bonding. Your goal may be a trained pet, but the ultimate payoff is far greater.

Chapter 3
Barking

Despite learning basic good manners, some dogs may engage in a bad habit from time to time, or they may exhibit an unwanted behavior that is a bit more difficult to tackle. For example, barking is a natural canine behavior that can easily get out of hand. Some barking is a good thing, and no one wants a dog who never makes a peep. On the other hand, excessive barking is one of the most common reasons for complaints about dogs.

WHY DOGS BARK

It's easy to tell when your dog is barking too much, but there are many possible reasons for it depending on the situation and his temperament. An excitable dog might be more prone to bark when he's happy, while a naturally suspicious dog will be intent on warning you of potential intruders. Either way, reform requires recognizing the underlying reasons.

Once you understand what is causing your dog to bark, use a combination of distraction, reward, and reinforcement to offer him a different behavior choice to replace the excessive barking.

TYPES OF BARKING AND HOW TO MANAGE THEM

Here are some steps you can take to figure out what type of barker your dog is. Keep a record of his barking habits for one week. Ask yourself:

- What prompted the barking, and what stopped it?
- How long did it last?
- Did it sound aggressive, happy, angry, or fearful?
- Was it accompanied by specific body language like tail wagging and jumping, or was it accompanied by raised hackles, a sign of fear or anger? (Hackles are the hairs on the back of the dog's neck.)

Once you have identified what prompts your dog's excessive barking, you can use one of the following methods to manage it.

ANTICIPATION BARKING

Signs

High pitched and constant, anticipation barking is often accompanied by jumping, spinning, and dashing around in anticipation of something good, like a walk or play session.

Management Technique

- Remain calm and quiet in these situations. Yanking your dog's collar or yelling at him will only add to his excitement.
- Make sure that your dog has enough exercise. Excess energy is a common cause of excitable barking. He should also be basic obedience trained. (See Chapter 2.)
- If your dog normally barks when visitors arrive, isolating him will increase his frenzy. Put him on a leash in the same room so that he can see everyone. Give him the *take a nap* command (see Chapter 2) and ignore him. A chew toy can also be an effective distraction. Any attention may encourage more barking. This includes looking at him or touching him.

QuickTip

Most dogs find it difficult to bark while lying down, so the *down* command often puts a stop to unwarranted barking.

DEMAND BARKING

Signs

Demand barking is often reinforced either unconsciously or deliberately by the owner to keep a dog quiet, but it has the opposite effect. If your dog stands by the door barking and you jump to open it, he will probably bark louder next time. This type of barking is hard to stop because it gives a dog control over his owner and environment.

Management Technique

- Instead of rewarding demand barking by reacting to it, ignore it.
- Teach a new response to replace demand barking, such as sitting on command or retrieving a toy—which also keeps his mouth occupied.

DidYouKnow?

The *Speak* and *Enough* Commands

You can teach your dog to bark on command to stop excessive barking. Say "Speak" and knock on a hard surface to get your dog to bark, and when he stops, immediately say "Enough" and reward him with a treat. This teaches him that bringing a noise to your attention is acceptable, but continued barking is not.

- Maintain a structured routine instead of responding to your dog's demands for food or walks. Offer your dog his food and toys only when he's polite and quiet rather than loud and demanding.

BOREDOM AND LONELINESS BARKING

Signs

Chronic barking to relieve boredom and loneliness is often combined with other obsessive habits, like digging or chewing. You must be persistent to break the cycle of this self-rewarding response.

Management Technique

- Maintain a structured daily routine and ensure that your dog has regular opportunities for play and socializing. A dog walker or doggy day care program can provide more social interactions if you're stuck at work for most of the day.
- Prevent situations that trigger boredom barking, such as access to looking out of a window or extensive time spent alone outside.
- Provide your dog with plenty of stimulating toys, like the ones made by Nylabone, to keep him occupied in your absence.

SELF-PROTECTION AND ANXIETY BARKING

Signs

High-pitched, defensive barking is meant to keep threats at a distance. It can go on for several minutes, sometimes accompanied

If your dog barks excessively when left alone outdoors, he is likely bored and lonely.

by other signs of anxiety like cowering, pacing, shaking, and drooling. Trying to calm your dog will rarely help, and dogs in this apprehensive state may bite. Crating him or isolating him to stop the barking may intensify the anxiety.

Management Technique
- Identify your dog's fear and avoid exposing him to it. If that isn't possible, distract your dog with food or play when his barking commences.
- Help your dog overcome his fear through gradual, positive introductions conducted at a pace he can handle. Reward calmness and never force him into situations that frighten him. If he becomes fearful, act nonchalant. Only he can decide that something doesn't pose a threat.

WARNING BARKING

Signs
Dogs normally bark to warn their pack of potential dangers. This can be directed at people, other animals, or any disturbance in the environment. Most dogs stop when they realize that there's no threat, but some dogs overreact to potential threats or have trouble distinguishing between important and minor events for reasons ranging from individual temperament to inadequate socialization.

Distract Your Dog From Barking

Loud reprimands are likely to make a barking dog even more anxious and aroused. Instead, distract him to interrupt his barking as soon as it starts. Call him, ask him to sit, throw a ball, or give him a chew toy to keep his mouth occupied.

If certain things constantly prompt barking, systematically interrupt your dog as soon as he starts and reward him for being quiet. For instance, if he normally barks every time he sees your neighbors in the backyard, distract him with a chew toy whenever the neighbors appear.

Make Easy

Once you understand what is causing your dog to bark, use a combination of distraction, reward, and reinforcement to offer him a different behavior to replace the excessive barking.

Management Technique

- After your dog sounds a warning to alert you, assure him that everything is okay, and insist that he quiet down.
- If your dog has trouble calming down after you assure him it's ok, give him the *take a nap* command or distract his attention with praise, a toy, or treats.

If you practice these steps consistently you should get results in three to four weeks.

If nothing seems to stop your dog's barking, chances are you're using the wrong approach. Reexamine the cause, provide a replacement behavior, and always reward him for being quiet.

Chapter 4
Begging

You can and should manage your dog's begging behavior, but no amount of training will prevent the instinctive canine response to look for tasty morsels. Since prehistory, dogs have been motivated to hang around humans in the hope of getting some food. This is a hardwired behavior that cannot be untaught.

WHY DOGS BEG

Puppies instinctively cry for food from the moment they are born. Their mother constantly reinforces this behavior by giving them milk and attention whenever they cry. Therefore, it's only natural for a puppy to continue using this successful strategy when he transitions to living with a human pack.

MANAGEMENT TECHNIQUES

If you want to eat dinner with your dog on your lap, that's your choice. But don't be surprised if he eventually starts helping himself to your food or pitches a fit when you suddenly decide that he shouldn't sit at the table. You cannot blame your dog for reacting this way—you made the rules and then you changed them.

BE CONSISTENT

To manage begging behavior, it's essential that all family members reinforce consistent rules. Dogs devote a great deal of time and effort to discovering new ways to procure tasty treats, and they seemingly have a sixth sense when it comes to soliciting food. If one family member persists in feeding the dog at the table, the pattern will instantly be reinforced.

IGNORE UNWANTED BEGGING

Your dog must understand exactly what behavior is acceptable and what isn't during mealtime. If you prefer to have your dog sit under the table (or at the table) while you eat, he can certainly do this without lunging, whining, drooling, or staring at you.

Ignore unwanted behavior and occasionally reward your dog for sitting quietly. This could be a pat on the head, a dog treat, or yes, even a taste of your food, but *only* when he's polite and well behaved and only when

To prevent begging, do not feed your dog from the table.

you decide to do this. If his pushy, demanding behavior never succeeds, he will have no reason to continue it. Dogs are very sensible this way; they pursue the course of action that gets results. You should also make sure that your dog is fed, exercised, and occupied with a chew toy before you sit down to eat. Chew toys, like the ones made by Nylabone, offer a great way to encourage positive behavior and enhance overall physical and mental fitness.

QuickTip

Because it's a survival instinct, dogs effortlessly learn and remember information related to procuring food. Giving in to you dog's begging only reinforces this behavior, so don't do it.

Trash Foraging

Many dogs try foraging in the trash when begging no longer gets results.
- Always keep the trash out of reach.
- Invest in a dog-proof trash container.
- Deposit trash in outdoor containers as frequently as possible to reduce temptation.

Make Easy

CONFINE YOUR DOG

Of course, some people prefer not to share their mealtime with a dog. In that case, ask your dog to go to his bed for a nap. (See Chapter 2.) If he ignores this request, reinforce the idea by leaving occasional treats on his bed. Finding them will have the same effect as successful begging. He will go back looking for more and be much more inclined to hang around that area. The clicker is another excellent reinforcement tool in this situation. Click and give a treat when he stays in his bed.

DIVIDE YOUR DOG'S DAILY FOOD RATION

If your dog customarily begs for his food, try dividing his daily food ration into more frequent meals to ensure that he isn't overly hungry by your mealtime. Also, feed your dog on a consistent schedule because erratic mealtimes can encourage begging.

Behavior modification to stop begging usually takes about three weeks. During this time, don't be surprised if your dog begins to complain loudly or resorts to some other attention-getting tactic. No matter what he tries, ignore it. Once he realizes that it doesn't work, it will stop.

Chapter 5
Chewing

It's normal for puppies to chew things, but it's a mistake to assume that this is a habit your dog will outgrow. For most dogs, chewing remains high on their list of favorite recreational activities. Certain breeds, like retrievers, are noted for being extremely interested in chewing throughout their lives.

WHY DOGS CHEW

Dogs use their mouths to explore and understand their environment. Random chewing may signify curiosity and a desire to investigate, as well as inadequate attention and spotty supervision. Chewing helps relieve teething pains. It can also relieve mental anxiety because the process releases endorphins to ease stress. To correct destructive chewing, you must treat the underlying motivation along with the behavior.

Puppies typically become fixated on chewing when they're teething, at around four months of age. Although younger puppies are equally apt to put things in their mouths and chew, their destructive ability improves as they gain jaw power and an adult set of choppers. In addition to damaging your home and belongings, uncontrolled chewing can lead to poisoning, intestinal obstructions, and mouth injuries.

MANAGEMENT TECHNIQUES

The following are some steps you can take to control chewing behavior.

REDIRECT THE CHEWING

Rather than trying to discourage your dog from chewing, redirect it to suitable objects. Teaching a dog to do something is always easier than trying to prevent him from doing something. Puppy proofing and careful supervision will prevent most destructive chewing, but it's inevitable that your dog will latch onto things he shouldn't chew.

PROVIDE APPROPRIATE CHEW TOYS

Food-dispensing toys, treat cubes, and puzzle toys will sustain the interest of most chewers, but you may need to experiment to discover what most appeals to your dog. Chew toys won't solve anything if your dog won't chew them. They must be appealing as well as safe. No matter what they are

Rather than trying to discourage your dog from chewing, redirect the behavior to suitable objects such as safe chew toys.

made of, they should be large and sturdy enough to prevent him from chewing off and ingesting small pieces.

Every dog has different chewing preferences and varying tendencies to chew things up and swallow them. Some dogs love stuffed toys and rubber squeaky toys, and they chew these for hours without actually making holes in them. Other dogs can chomp right through a giant chew toy. You can ask breeders for recommendations on which toys are best for your breed, but there is no such thing as a 100-percent safe dog toy. The only way to know what's safe for your dog is to supervise him while he chews. If you're worried that he may eat the toy or choke on it, take it away.

When you discover what your dog loves, keep plenty of great chew toys on hand for him. However, don't make them all available. Rotating his toys will maintain his interest in them. He will lose interest if they're always lying around the house. Put them away, switch them around, bring out new ones occasionally, and always discard any that show excessive wear.

TRADE FOR SUITABLE TOYS

When you discover your dog chewing something he shouldn't have, remove the item from his mouth. Don't scold him because he will have no idea what he's being scolded for. Worse yet, this may discourage him from chewing anything in your presence, which defeats the purpose of chew training. This approach may also encourage him to steal objects and hide them for later chewing. If he's chewing to relieve anxiety, reprimanding him may also intensify the behavior rather than stopping it. Instead, exchange the item for something he's allowed to chew. When you see him happily gnawing away on that, praise him.

PLAY WITH YOUR DOG

Play with your dog regularly to reinforce his understanding of boundaries and provide sufficient mental and physical exercise. Every dog is different in this regard. Dogs of the same age and breed may require different amounts of attention and exercise. As mentioned earlier, provide a wide variety of interesting chew toys, like the ones made by Nylabone, to prevent him from getting bored in your absence.

Redirect and reinforce chew rules from the moment your new puppy arrives. By the time he starts teething, he will develop definite preferences for his favorite chew toys rather than the leg of the dining room table. But don't expect this to happen overnight. Puppies have short attention spans and need frequent reminders of the rules. Supervision is essential until your puppy is old enough to understand and remember this concept. For some puppies this may take six months; for others it can take two years.

QuickTip

If you want your dog to chew something, put a dab of butter, peanut butter, or cream cheese on it to get him interested. If you want him to stay away, a bitter apple spray is often an effective chewing deterrent.

Choose the Right Chew Toy

Most dogs retain a lifetime interest in chewing, but they possess an excellent ability to single out individual items to chew. They also become more discriminating about their chewing preferences as they mature. You can encourage this through play.

- Put a mixture of items on the floor, and encourage your dog to investigate them.
- When he chooses one, use a clicker to tell him he has picked up the right one (a chew toy) or stop him if he chooses the wrong one (your new leather glove). You will be amazed at how quickly he learns the difference.

NYLABONE

Make Easy

Chapter 6
Digging

All dogs like to dig to some extent, but it's far more likely to become an ingrained habit for certain breeds, like terriers and Dachshunds, who perceive digging as part of their job.

Unfortunately, digging will not only ruin your lawn, but this habit is also easily transitioned to rugs, chair cushions, and mattresses. Because it's inherent and self-rewarding, it's also self-perpetuating, making it tough to revise. If you allow your puppy to dig to his heart's content for months, you face a much bigger challenge trying to stop this habit when he's older.

Why Dogs Dig

There are many reasons why dogs dig, and you must identify the motivation to modify the behavior.

BURYING VALUABLES

Signs

Wolves, the ancestors of dogs, instinctively hoard food by hiding it in holes dug in dirt or snow with their front paws. They drop their treasure into the hole and use their noses to fill it in. Dogs have inherited this hardwired behavior pattern, and they perform it precisely the same way. In addition to food, they bury toys, socks, or anything else they consider valuable.

If your dog happens to be outdoors when he decides to hide something valuable, he will dig a hole. Indoors, he may hide it under your pillows or between the couch cushions. Along with the surprise of finding an old pizza crust buried under your pillow, furniture can be damaged by this repetitive poking and pawing.

Management Technique

Because this behavior is instinctive, supervision is the only way to control it. You can also provide your dog with a designated digging area in which to hide his valuables. Indoors, a big blanket in a crate often works well. Outdoors, either allocate an area of your yard for digging or provide your dog with his own sandbox to play in.

Digging can be a sign of boredom, loneliness, excessive heat, or a desire to escape—or it can just be something your dog does for fun.

ESCAPING HEAT OR FINDING SAFETY

Signs

If stressed by the heat or other factors, your dog may dig a hole in which to hide or find comfort.

Management Technique

Whenever your dog is outdoors, make sure that he has a safe, comfortable spot in which to lie down, as well as plenty of shade and water. If that doesn't stop him from digging, try restricting him to a hard surface like a patio or deck for a few weeks. If his digging is due to anxiety when left alone outside, you will need to identify and remove the source of his fear or change his routine entirely—including reducing the amount of time he's left alone outdoors.

BOREDOM

Signs

If your dog regularly digs in specific areas, like flowerbeds, this may be due to boredom. Instead of being provided

The Doggy Sandbox

A doggy digging area can range from a dedicated corner of your yard filled with loose dirt or sand to an elaborate sandbox. To be effective it should be at least 1 foot (30 cm) longer than your dog's body length from nose to rump. This ensures that it's big enough for your dog to have fun burying and excavating his valuables.

- Bury some of your dog's favorite toys and a few treats to get him interested in this spot.
- Dogs are excellent at discriminating details. When your dog digs in this area, encourage him with clicker reinforcement or a special command like "Dig."
- Even when your dog begins to regularly use his digging spot, supervise him carefully. You will probably need to redirect him to his sandbox a few times to reinforce the idea that he can dig here only.

Make Easy

with stimulation by playing with his toys or with you, he's finding his own entertainment.

Management Technique

Restrict your dog's access to these areas. If he begins excavating a new spot, stopping him from digging really won't solve the problem unless you're prepared to supervise him constantly whenever he's in the yard. A better approach is to stop leaving him outside alone. Find a way to relieve his boredom through a more structured routine and plenty of daily mental and physical stimulation.

TRYING TO ESCAPE

Signs

Initially, digging to escape an enclosed area can be prompted by excess energy, boredom, natural curiosity, roaming instincts, or loneliness. Regardless of the reason, if a dog succeeds in escaping once, he is much more likely to try it again.

Management Technique

Reinforce fencing by sinking barriers 1 foot (30 cm) underground along fence perimeters or by placing at least 1 foot (30 cm) of mesh or paving along the bottom of the fence.

For some dogs, constantly running away from you in a large fenced-in yard can encourage the desire to escape. When outdoors, regularly encourage your dog to come when called and reward this response.

QuickTip

Screening or mesh covered by a few inches (several centimeters) of dirt or mulch can discourage dogs from digging.

HUNTING

Signs

A dog with a strong predatory instinct is hardwired to dig for rodents, and you can't fault him for doing his job. When he detects the scent of burrowing animals, it may be impossible to discourage his digging instinct.

To prevent digging, supervise your dog when he is outdoors.

Whenever your dog starts digging, you can divert his attention with a toy he likes or by playing a game.

Management Technique

Professional pest control is the best way to rid your lawn of moles or other burrowing creatures. (Do-it-yourself pest control methods often contain poisons that can be hazardous to pets.) You can also restrict his access to these areas.

Digging is a natural canine behavior rooted in a dog's basic survival instinct. It can be managed by making modifications to his environment, but supervision is the most effective way to prevent it.

DidYouKnow?

Neutering may help discourage a male dog's desire to roam, but if it is already an established habit, don't expect this to instantly solve the problem. You must also invest in good fencing and provide behavior modification.

Chapter 7

Jumping Up

Not only is jumping up an annoying canine behavior, but it can also be dangerous. Large dogs can cause the most problems by actually knocking someone down when they jump. But small dogs also resort to this strategy when they feel frustrated and ignored. Uncontrolled jumping can escalate into scratching, barking, and nipping to demand attention.

WHY DOGS JUMP

Jumping is an instinctive canine behavior. Puppies start bouncing on each other as soon as they can walk, and it quickly becomes one of their favorite play activities. Not only do dogs find it fun, but it's also a great way to get attention. Most of the time, it's harmless. Of course, there will be occasions when you don't want your dog jumping up to say hello. It's up to you to teach him when it's not okay to engage in this behavior.

MANAGEMENT TECHNIQUES

Many training guides advise stepping on a dog's toes, kneeing him in the chest, or jerking his leash to discourage him from jumping. In addition to the possibility of injury, these negative methods usually get limited results. Dogs jump to solicit attention, and for many, even a negative response from you qualifies as acceptable attention. Any response—whether it is verbal, physical, or even eye contact—may reinforce the pattern.

Another common suggestion is to ignore your dog whenever he jumps. But many dogs simply love jumping—that in and of itself is enough of a reward. If you turn your back, they will just happily jump onto your back.

Various methods may discourage jumping, but they will only be effective if your dog consistently receives the same response from every single human he jumps on. Although you may tell him not to jump hundreds of times, invariably he will get a hug, pat, or taste of ice cream from someone else he jumps on. And at that point, his behavior is reinforced and the training process must begin all over again. In reality, it's best to discourage your dog from jumping up on people altogether. When all is said and done, only your dog can decide that jumping isn't worth the effort.

Regardless of size, a dog who jumps on people is a nuisance and potentially dangerous. Teach your dog not to jump up unless invited to do so.

REWARD AN ALTERNATE RESPONSE

The best way to prevent the jumping habit is to consistently reward an alternate response. For example, reward your dog for sitting or standing calmly to greet you. Never acknowledge him when he jumps on you. Not only must you never praise a jump, but your entire family and all visitors mustn't either.

INTERRUPT THE JUMPING

You can also consistently interrupt your dog's jumping behavior before it happens. Before he jumps he will probably make eye contact and shift his weight to his back legs. When you spot these telltale clues, get a hand on his collar before he can follow through. Follow this up immediately with a command like the *sit*, and reward that response. Timing is very important when giving this alternate command. For some dogs, a clicker is the easiest way to reinforce it quickly. Don't take your hand off of his collar until you're sure that he has calmed down and his desire to jump has been redirected.

If your dog is more exuberant, you may need to start this retraining by holding his collar and interrupting him mid-flight. As soon as he starts rearing up, take his collar, tell him to sit, and reward that response. If your dog is only 8 inches (20 cm) tall, you may need to get down to his level for effective eye contact and communication when doing this. When dealing with a very exuberant dog, be sure to praise him in a low-key manner so that he doesn't become overexcited and jump again.

When rewarding your dog for not jumping, your goal is to keep him happy but calm. For instance, some dogs go crazy for food treats, and it may be impossible to control his desire to jump when he sees food. In that case, use a less exciting reward, like petting or a toy, until he starts to learn some self-control.

Quick Tip

Teach your dog jumping tricks to give him an outlet for excess energy and a way to gain positive attention by showing off his jumping skills.

TRAIN YOUR DOG TO JUMP ON COMMAND

If you prefer, you can use the reverse approach and train your dog to jump on command. This gives him a cue to know when it's okay to jump. Use a command like "Up" or "Jump" and a special gesture like an upraised hand. Have an alternate command to let him know when he should keep four feet on the floor. Dogs are very good at interpreting human cues, and the right response should always merit a reward. Most dogs learn this concept quickly as long as you provide a consistent message backed up with plenty of positive reinforcement.

Be prepared to train your dog not to jump for at least three weeks to change his behavior. Some dogs will respond during this time frame, while others will need more time and attention.

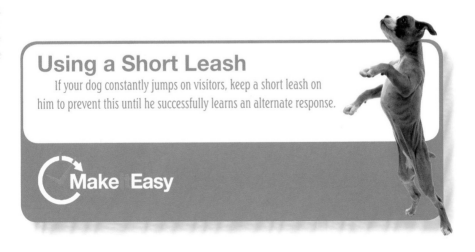

Using a Short Leash

If your dog constantly jumps on visitors, keep a short leash on him to prevent this until he successfully learns an alternate response.

Make Easy

Chapter 8
Leash Pulling

A leisurely stroll with your dog is one of life's great pleasures. Needless to say, to thoroughly enjoy it, he must contentedly walk at *your* pace on a loose lead.

Why Dogs Pull

Dogs easily learn habits such as pulling, lagging, and trotting in every direction during a walk because these behaviors are reinforced by cues and rewards in their environment. If your dog sniffs something interesting but you want to keep walking, he will slow down and lag or stop completely. If he sees another dog across the street, he will speed up and lunge ahead. In either case, you probably respond by stopping or changing direction to satisfy him. Before you know it, you have a dog who constantly lags, lunges, and winds his leash around your legs like a corkscrew.

Likewise, owners of small dogs often assume that it's okay to allow them to pull to their hearts' content when they're wearing a harness. Although the dog isn't going to choke as he would if he was wearing a collar, pulling should *not* be encouraged. Situations will arise when you must quickly get your dog under control for safety reasons. This will be much harder if he's accustomed to forging ahead on his leash, oblivious to you.

Management Techniques

We are usually so intent on teaching puppies to walk on leash that we fail to notice budding bad habits like lunging and lagging. After a dog is accustomed to behaving this way during a walk, it can be difficult to correct these habits. In the past, most training books recommended using leash corrections to stop a dog from pulling ahead or lagging behind. However, this is one more situation in which positive reinforcement is much more effective and much less tedious.

REINFORCE POLITE LEASH HABITS

It's very easy for bad on-leash habits to form. However, it's also very easy to incorporate polite leash habits into basic leash training. Always reward your dog using treats, praise, or a clicker when he walks at your pace on a loose lead. Consistently let him know that this is the response—the only response—that you want. Dogs easily become distracted and excited by all the interesting sights, sounds, and smells around them. Regularly make

A dog who pulls on leash is difficult to control and poses a danger to himself and the person walking him.

eye contact with your dog during a walk to ensure that he remains focused on your training message. He isn't going to learn anything unless he's paying attention to you.

INTERRUPT THE PULLING BEHAVIOR

Dogs are sensitive to the pressure of the leash. Keep a slight tension on the leash at all times. It should never be taut, nor should it be completely loose. When your dog starts to stray from your side, simply stop moving altogether. When he responds, immediately make eye contact and reward this behavior with praise and a treat.

It's always better to interrupt him by halting your forward progress before he veers off course, so pay attention to potential distractions while you're walking. Also, never jerk, pull, or drag your dog. Smaller dogs can suffer neck or throat injuries this way, but dogs of any size will develop an aversion to the leash if they are forcefully dragged along.

WALK YOUR DOG WHEN HE'S CALM

Never start walking if your dog is in a wild frenzy. Dogs normally do the dance of joy at walk time, which often translates into jumping and lunging when they get outside. Insist that your dog sit calmly when you put his leash on. If he starts to drag you out the door, stop and wait until he's calm and collected.

If he suddenly begins pulling or lunging and you lose control, just stop and wait. Don't acknowledge him, which may get him even more excited. More importantly, don't let him gain the reward he's seeking by dragging you across the street after a squirrel. Trying to reel him in like a fish on a lure will only encourage his reflexive response to pull even harder in the opposite direction. It's more effective to stop and wait for him to realize that this behavior brings his walk to a screeching halt. At that point, abruptly turn and begin walking him in the opposite direction. Make eye contact, praise him calmly, and reward him for heeling politely.

ALLOW WANDERING WHEN APPROPRIATE

You can also teach your dog a special command to let him know when it's okay to wander out to the end of the leash and explore. But never forget to reward him when he comes back to your side.

QuickTip

If you have trouble getting control of your dog before a walk, teach him to sit when you are putting on his leash.

If you consistently discourage your dog from pulling and reward him for walking nicely, you should see notable improvements within three weeks.

Halters and Harnesses

A halter or head harness can discourage many serious leash pullers. The leash attaches to a ring under the dog's chin, which prevents him from using his chest and shoulders to pull. A dog's chest and shoulders contain some of his strongest muscles, which explains the resistance you get when you pull your collared dog in one direction and he resists. Wearing a halter or harness makes it harder for him to forge ahead, and his only comfortable option will be walking at your side at a moderate pace.

- Make sure that the halter (or harness) is properly fitted so that your dog cannot slip out of it.
- Let your dog get used to wearing the halter (or harness) for an hour or two for at least three days before attaching the leash.
- Start leash training him to the halter (or harness) in a safe, fenced area rather than a public street. Don't take him out walking until he feels comfortable and accepts wearing it.

Make Easy

Chapter 9
Mouthing and Biting

Puppies are not born with an innate understanding that it's wrong to bite hard. Luckily, the majority of them learn this crucial lesson before they have a full set of teeth. A puppy's teeth start to emerge at three to four weeks of age, which is also when socialization begins through play with his mother and littermates. Much of this play involves experimental biting and nipping. If a puppy bites too hard, his mother reprimands him with an immediate nip or growl, or his littermates refuse to play with him. This concept is reinforced through weeks of daily interaction. By 12 weeks of age, most puppies have a pretty good understanding of bite control.

Why Dogs Mouth and Bite

All dogs have the ability to moderate bite pressure, and puppies begin learning this at a very early age. But that doesn't mean that they stop experimenting with nipping and biting. Dogs of all ages use their mouths to explore their environment, and this includes experimenting on their human companions. Your puppy will probably sniff your hand, lick it, and then try a tentative nibble. If you allow him to think that nibbling is okay, he will do it again—maybe a little harder next time. Before you know it, he will have decided that your hand makes a great chew toy.

Management Techniques

Nipping is a normal part of dog play, but an accidental hard nip will elicit an immediate negative response from a canine playmate. To some extent, this concept applies to play with human playmates, but the rules are just a little different. Rather than moderating his biting, he needs to learn that using his teeth on your skin is never okay under any circumstances.

Interact with Your Dog Daily

Appropriate daily interaction is the best way to prevent your dog from getting into the habit of hard biting and nipping. Unfortunately, if he's already in the habit of doing so, people will tend to avoid playing with him. As a result, he will get few opportunities to learn what constitutes acceptable play behavior.

Play with your dog every day for at least 15 minutes. Try not to get him too wound up during these sessions. He is much more likely to accidentally nip

Although nipping is a normal part of canine play, you must teach your dog that using his teeth on your skin is never okay under any circumstances.

hard if he becomes overly excited. Your goal is to teach him focus and self-control. After a few play sessions, it will become easier for you to predict which games or gestures are likely to trigger a playing frenzy and a possible nip. Your objective is to keep him at a level where he can control his actions and respond to you.

COMMUNICATE THAT MOUTHING HURTS

If and when your dog accidentally nips you during play, instantly let him know that it hurts (whether or not it really does). Tell him "No biting" or "Be gentle," and end the play session immediately. Scolding him will only get him more excited or put him on the defensive, which may lead to more biting rather than less. If you end the play session because of a nip, your dog will learn that mouthing has consequences, and he will eventually stop doing it. Mimicking a painful canine yelp may also convey the proper message to a biting dog.

✓**QuickTip**

Never allow your dog to tug your pant leg, nibble your shoe, or mouth your jewelry. These behaviors make it harder for him to understand the limits of acceptable play with humans.

SUPERVISE PLAY WITH OTHER DOGS

Puppies learn bite control from playing with other dogs. However, this may not be a good idea if your dog already has serious biting issues. A play session can potentially escalate into a fight unless both participants understand the boundaries of acceptable dog play. Until your dog's social skills improve, supervise his play with other dogs to ensure that it remains on safe, friendly terms.

Most puppies learn to moderate their bite pressure by three months of age. However, an adult or a puppy over four months of age can take quite a while to become conditioned to this idea. At times, behavior modification may seem frustratingly slow, but you can be sure that this problem will only intensify if you ignore it.

Hand Feeding Your Dog

Teaching your dog to gently take food from your hand provides an excellent lesson in bite control.

- Sit on the floor holding an irresistible treat in your open palm. If your dog grabs for it, close your hand and tell him to be gentle. After 10 or 20 attempts, he will probably become confused and sit to think about the situation. That's when you tell him he's a good boy and give him a treat—but from your other hand.
- If you're dealing with a dog who has virtually no bite control, begin this training by offering treats from a metal spoon rather than using your hands and fingers. Most dogs do not like the taste of metal, which will also help discourage them from snatching the morsel. When your dog tries to grab the treat, give him a verbal warning and lift it out of his reach. When he's gentle, allow him to have it and follow up with praise.
- Once he learns to politely take a treat off of the spoon, begin offering them from your hand. Some dogs require daily practice for months to reliably learn this concept.

Make Easy

Chapter 10
Not Coming When Called

An astounding number of problem behaviors are minimized or eliminated entirely if your dog reliably comes when called. If you can rely on him to do so, it's much easier to monitor his behavior and prevent him from getting into things that he shouldn't. It's also much easier to ensure that he gets plenty of exercise if he can be allowed off the leash to run and play. If your dog consistently ignores you or refuses to come when called, the freedom of off-leash exercise becomes out of the question for safety reasons, and your daily routine is filled with needless complications. Simply persuading your dog to come into the house before you go to work can turn into a major project.

WHY DOGS DON'T COME WHEN CALLED

Inconsistent or incomplete training is the usual reason why dogs fail to come when called. Your puppy may happily come bounding into the kitchen at dinnertime, but that doesn't necessarily guarantee that he'll respond with equal enthusiasm when he's off lead playing with his friends at the dog park. Another reason why a dog may not come reliably is because he has been summoned in the past for reasons he considers unpleasant, like a bath or nail trimming.

MANAGEMENT TECHNIQUES

If you have already made some training mistakes and your dog responds to the *come* command by diving under the bed, you must revise this negative association. This may require three or four weeks of daily practice.

If your dog becomes less responsive at any point during the training, don't keep repeating the command or lose your temper. Even if you don't raise your voice, your body language and facial expression can reveal your impatience.

TEACH THE *COME* COMMAND AGAIN

If your dog is not responding to the *come* command, you may have to start teaching it from scratch.

- Work in a small, secure area so that your dog doesn't have the option of running off or ignoring you.

Practice the *Come* Command

Constantly reward coming when called even if your dog seems to respond perfectly when you call him. When you're practicing with him in a secure and enclosed indoor area, arrange for potential distractions. For instance, ask someone to orchestrate some well-timed kitchen/dinner noises, or walk into the room with a snack. Your dog may not respond to your command instantly in a situation like this, but do your best to encourage him. Dogs confront an infinite number of potential distractions, and they make a conscious choice every time they decide to come when called. Make eye contact and reward any indication that he's making the right choice by coming to you. Slowly add bigger distractions as his response becomes more reliable.

Make Easy

- With your dog at your side, get down to his level, make eye contact, and ask for a *come* in a soft, encouraging voice. Reward him with a treat as soon as he looks at you. Repeat this 20 times for the first lesson.
- For the next lesson, begin with the same procedure, but after giving your dog a few treats, move a few steps away from him. Very likely, he won't think twice about coming to you in this situation.
- Practice this daily, gradually moving a few paces away each day. When your dog has a good grasp of this concept, briskly walk away from him and give the *come* command. When he follows you, stop and reward him.
- Each day, move away from your dog a bit farther and faster. Always have a treat ready when he responds.

For some dogs it helps to reinforce the vocal command with a distinctive sound such as a click or a whistle. Be creative; try shaking a box of dog treats to lure him in. You can also use gestures to reinforce the concept, but for this particular aspect of training, a vocal command is essential in many situations. Use whatever method your dog responds to best—but consistently use the same word and gesture, and make sure that it's always fun for him.

DON'T CALL FOR UNPLEASANT TASKS

Never ask your dog to come to you for something he isn't going to like, and never use his name in these situations. If he dreads a bath or nail trimming, round him up rather than calling him for these chores. Most importantly, never ask him to come when you're angry or planning to scold him. If you do, your dog will think of the *come* command as something negative and will hide from you or ignore you completely.

Because inconsistent or incomplete training are the usual reasons why dogs fail to come when called, retraining your dog to come reliably will take longer in that you're now revising a habit rather than teaching a new one. Your dog may start coming when called within a few weeks, but it may require months of practice before you can dependably allow him off leash outdoors. Consistently encourage and reward him for coming to you in a wide range of situations. Some dogs are more easily distracted, others respond less readily to praise, and some are just slower to respond. Despite these variables, every dog can be taught to reliably come when called.

QuickTip

To reinforce coming when called, use whatever type of reward elicits an immediate positive response from your dog: petting, praise, food, or a toy.

Inconsistent or incomplete training is the usual reason why dogs fail to come when called.

Chapter 11
When All Else Fails

Occasionally, a problem behavior defies the most dedicated training efforts. These behaviors can vary from chewing issues to complicated personality issues like shyness or aggression. They often become apparent when a dog reaches adolescence and intensify as he matures. The end result can be a very discouraged dog owner. In these cases, expert advice can provide a multitude of options.

When to Get Help

We all have a few quirks, including our dogs. Because we love them, it can be challenging to recognize when canine misbehavior moves beyond quirkiness and requires professional assistance.

To figure out if you require the services of a dog trainer, ask yourself the following questions:

- *Has the problem behavior led to drastic modifications of your lifestyle?* Example: Your dog's extreme separation anxiety makes it increasingly difficult to leave him alone for any length of time.
- *Does the problem behavior pose a potential danger to people or other pets?* Example: Your rambunctious puppy has morphed into a bully and has begun to terrorize other dogs at the dog park, or worse, you don't feel safe having him in the same room with small children.
- *Has the problem behavior compromised your dog's ability to function normally?* Example: Your dog's timidity has worsened to the point where he's fearful of any dog or person he meets.

Why You Should Get Help

Many problem behaviors are the result of long-term habits that have been overlooked or tolerated. For instance, it's normal to expect puppies to outgrow rowdiness or hyperactivity. Without behavior modification, however, some overly energetic puppies may mature into completely unmanageable adults.

Some habits, such as chasing small animals or guarding territory, are inseparable from a breed's natural behavior. As the dog matures, these natural instincts intensify. Without consistent early training, it can be challenging to control them later on.

Unsuccessful or incomplete training can also lead to problems. A well-

Many problem behaviors are the result of long-term habits that have been overlooked or tolerated.

meaning owner may inadvertently reward the behavior she wants to discourage or make a problem worse by using the wrong approach to correct it.

Many dogs require more daily exercise and social interaction than they receive. Depriving dogs of necessary activity causes boredom and pent-up energy, which can lead to the dog developing problem behaviors to alleviate his lack of sufficient stimulation and restlessness.

Expert advice can help you identify the reasons for a problem behavior and design an effective strategy to revise it.

WHERE TO GET HELP

Professionals who can help you range from dog trainers to certified veterinary behaviorists. A skilled trainer can help you recognize and manage behavior issues before they become major problems, and training classes are the most common means of reforming these behaviors. Dogs typically learn basic commands (see Chapter 2), and owners are introduced to different training techniques and receive advice on basic behavior issues. Classes also provide excellent opportunities for socialization with dogs and humans, which can be equally important for many dogs.

Group training classes come in many forms, including the following.

PUPPY KINDERGARTEN

Classes are open to puppies under six months of age who have completed their series of puppy vaccinations. These programs familiarize puppies and owners with basic commands and positive social interactions in a structured setting. Owners also benefit from advice on issues like housetraining, puppy care and development, and canine communication.

Choosing a Behavior Consultant

When choosing a behavior consultant, it's your responsibility to evaluate their background and skills and choose the person best qualified to treat your dog. Here are a few qualities to look for:

- Academic background: Although most trainers and behavior consultants have professional credentials or certification, these are not requirements to become one. Regardless of academic background, behavior specialists should be thoroughly familiar with basic learning theory and its application in dog training.
- Practical experience: Trainers should have extensive working experience. This includes a comprehensive understanding of species-specific and breed-specific canine behavior, as well as a complete familiarity with training equipment and behavior modification techniques.
- Methodology: Training methods generally range from only positive reinforcement to a combination of correction and positive reinforcement. In either case, the advice should combine knowledge derived from personal training experience and scientifically valid concepts of animal behavior. It should never include vague generalized statements or secondhand information.
- Communication skills: Trainers should clearly explain the reasons for each particular step in the remedial training process so that you know what to expect. This includes a description of training methods that will be used, the number of consultations your pet may require, the cost of treatment (including phone consultations and follow-up visits), and most importantly, their predictions about its ultimate effectiveness. They should be friendly, patient, and willing to answer all of your questions, and they shouldn't make you feel foolish for asking them.

Make It Easy

FORMAL OBEDIENCE

Classes typically consist of weekly basic obedience training. Each week the instructor introduces a new command, such as *sit* or *come*, demonstrates the training technique, and assists owners as they train their dogs. Trainers may also suggest alternate training methods that are better suited to a particular dog's personality. Owners are expected to follow up each lesson with daily practice at home. Most dogs in these classes range in age from six months to a year, but they are open to dogs of all ages.

FAMILY DOG TRAINING

Classes follow the format of traditional obedience training with an added emphasis on how to utilize these training skills in typical situations that dog owners confront. They also focus on helping owners better understand and evaluate their dogs' behavior.

ADVANCED CLASSES

If you enjoy dog training and your dog reveals a natural talent for this work, you may want to look into more advanced training. The choices are many. Local kennel clubs and training groups usually offer specialized training in agility, obedience, tracking, or herding. Training your dog for an American Kennel Club (AKC) Good Citizen title is a good starting point. This is also the basic qualification required if you're interested in training your dog for therapy work.

PRIVATE INSTRUCTION AND BEHAVIOR CONSULTATION

Individual instruction may be the best choice if you feel that your dog requires intensive treatment for a serious problem like aggression, shyness, or phobias. The program may include a combination of phone consultations and private lessons at a training facility or your

If a particular problem behavior defies your dedicated training efforts, it may be best to seek the advice of a professional trainer.

home. This approach is usually more thorough, time consuming, and expensive.

The dog's typical routine and behavior will be closely evaluated. Family members will be interviewed at length to provide additional insight into the scope of the problem and possible contributing factors. The resulting recommendations may include a combination of remedial training, behavior modification techniques, and adjustments to the dog's environment and daily routine.

How Long Will It Take?

Dogs are highly adaptable and easily modify their behavior to changing circumstances. This has been the basis for their evolutionary success. Professional guidance can work wonders if you're dedicated to revising the problem behavior your dog is displaying. However, guidance from a trainer or behaviorist will be pointless unless you're willing to follow their treatment recommendations and consistently work with your dog. Be realistic about the time and effort you're prepared to devote to this before agreeing to a particular training program because it may take a lot of both to correct your dog's behavior.

Also, ask yourself the following questions:

- Is everyone in the family ready and willing to consistently follow these recommendations?
- Do you fully understand the suggested methods?
- Are you comfortable with them?
- Do you feel that you have the skill to follow through with certain aspects of a remedial training program?
- Most importantly, are you confident that this program is right for your dog?

Having answers to these questions will help reduce the amount of time and effort it takes to correct problem behaviors.

Training a dog is comparable to nurturing any other type of relationship. It requires patience, flexibility, and realistic expectations. It doesn't happen without some effort on your part, but it's well worth the unconditional love you will receive from your dog in return.

DidYouKnow?

Some serious problem behaviors, such as severe phobias, often respond well to drug therapy. Your veterinarian can refer you to a board-certified veterinary behaviorist for advice in this area.

QuickTip

A detailed log of your dog's activities often provides valuable insight into the underlying reasons for chronic misbehavior.

INDEX

About the Author

Freelance artist and writer **Amy Fernandez** has bred Chinese Cresteds since 1980. She has authored several books on canine care and breeding, including *Maltese*; *Poodles*; and *Dog Breeding as a Fine Art*, winner of the prestigious DWAA Presidential Award of Excellence. She also serves as Editor of *Xolo News* and writes for *Dog World*, *Popular Dogs*, *AKC Gazette*, *AKC Family Dog*, and *Dogs in Review*. Her *Dogs in Review* historical series is a three-time winner of the Elsworth Howell Award, 2006 winner of the Robert Cole Award, and 2008 APAW winner for best long feature article. She is former President of the Dog Writers Association of America and is currently President of the Xoloitzcuintli Club of America. You can visit Amy's website at www.amyfernandez.net.

Photo Credits

Adrov Andriy (Shutterstock): 50
Ankya (Shutterstock): 7
Annette (Shutterstock): 52
Joy Brown (Shutterstock): 10
Bryoni Castelijn (Shutterstock): 15
Costin Cojocaru (Shutterstock): 45
Tad Denson (Shutterstock): 41
Perry Harmon (Shutterstock): 27
Margo Harrison (Shutterstock): 36
IntraClique LLC (Shutterstock): 12
Eric Isselée (Shutterstock): 3, 16, 17, 22, 35, 37, 57, 59
Petr Jilek (Shutterstock): 24
Kezzu (Shutterstock): 21
Justin Kinney (Shutterstock): 34
Erik Lam (Shutterstock): 9, 27
Somer McCain (Shutterstock): 4
Kirk Peart Professional Imaging (Shutterstock): 56
Andrejs Pidjass (Shutterstock): 20
Shutterstock: 38
Ljupco Smokovski (Shutterstock): 42
Fernando Jose Vasconcelos Soares (Shutterstock): 6
Claudia Steininger (Shutterstock): 28
TFH Archives: 8, 18, 23, 30, 32, 37, 40, 48, 49, 53, 54, 58
April Turner (Shutterstock): 2
Jason Vandehey (Shutterstock): 26
Anke van Wyk (Shutterstock): 14
Zdorov Kirill Vladimirovich (Shutterstock): 2
Ivonne Wierink (Shutterstock): 44
Michael Zysman (Shutterstock): 46

Front cover: Anyka (Shutterstock); Jean Frooms (Shutterstock)
Back cover: iofoto (Shutterstock)